WAR OF THE FOXES

ALSO BY RICHARD SIKEN

Crush

RICHARD SIKEN
WAR OF THE FOXES

COPPER CANYON PRESS

PORT TOWNSEND, WASHINGTON

Printed in the United States of America

Cover art: David de las Heras, *La Nube Roja,* 2012.

Copper Canyon Press is in residence at Fort Worden State Park in Port Townsend, Washington, under the auspices of Centrum. Centrum is a gathering place for artists and creative thinkers from around the world, students of all ages and backgrounds, and audiences seeking extraordinary cultural enrichment.

LIBRARY OF CONGRESS CATALOGING-IN-PUBLICATION DATA

Siken, Richard, 1967–
  [Poems. Selections]
  War of the foxes / Richard Siken.
     pages ; cm

  ISBN 978-1-55659-477-9 (softcover : acid-free paper)
  I. Title.

PS3619.I48A6 2015
811'.6—dc23

                              2014032605

          98765

COPPER CANYON PRESS
Post Office Box 271
Port Townsend, Washington 98368
www.coppercanyonpress.org

MIX
Paper | Supporting
responsible forestry
FSC
www.fsc.org   FSC® C008955

ACKNOWLEDGMENTS

Grateful acknowledgment is made to the editors of the publications in which these poems, some in alternate versions, first appeared: *The Awl; BOAAT; BODY; Columbia Poetry Review; Cordite Poetry Review; Cue; Diagram; Fairy Tale Review; Forklift, Ohio; From the Fishouse; Gulf Coast Online; Indiana Review; Jubilat; New England Review; Psychology Tomorrow Magazine; Tin House;* and Poem-a-Day from the Academy of American Poets. The first section of "War of the Foxes" was included in the anthology *State of the Union: 50 Political Poems,* edited by Joshua Beckman and Matthew Zapruder, Wave Books, 2008.

CONTENTS

WAR OF THE FOXES

THE WAY THE LIGHT REFLECTS

The paint doesn't move the way the light reflects,
so what's there to be faithful to? *I am faithful
to you, darling.* I say it to the paint. The bird floats
in the unfinished sky with nothing to hold it.
The man stands, the day shines. His insides and
his outsides kept apart with an imaginary line—
thick and rude and imaginary because there is
no separation, fallacy of the local body, paint
on paint. I have my body and you have yours.
Believe it if you can. Negative space is silly.
When you bang on the wall you have to remember
you're on both sides of it already but go ahead,
yell at yourself. Some people don't understand
anything. They see the man but not the light,
they see the field but not the varnish. There is no
light in the paint, so how can you argue with them?
They are probably right anyway. I paint in his face
and I paint it out again. There is a question
I am afraid to ask: *to supply the world with what?*

LANDSCAPE WITH A BLUR OF CONQUERORS

To have a thought, there must be an object—
the field is empty, sloshed with gold, a hayfield thick
with sunshine. There must be an object so land
a man there, solid on his feet, on solid ground, in
a field fully flooded, enough light to see him clearly,

the light on his skin and bouncing off his skin.
He's easy to desire since there's not much to him,
vague and smeary in his ochers, in his umbers,
burning in the open field. Forget about his insides,
his plumbing and his furnaces, put a thing in his hand

and be done with it. No one wants to know what's
in his head. It should be enough. To make something
beautiful should be enough. It isn't. It should be.
The smear of his head—I paint it out, I paint it in
again. I ask it what it wants. *I want to be a cornerstone,*

says the head. *Let's kill something.* Land a man in a
landscape and he'll try to conquer it. Make him
handsome and you're a fascist, make him ugly and
you're saying nothing new. The conqueror suits up
and takes the field, his horse already painted in

beneath him. What do you do with a man like that?
While you are deciding, more men ride in. The hand
sings *weapon.* The mind says *tool.* The body swerves
in the service of the mind, which is evidence of
the mind but not actual proof. More conquerors.

They swarm the field and their painted flags unfurl.
Crown yourself with leaves and stake your claim
before something smears up the paint. I turned away
from darkness to see daylight, to see what would
happen. What happened? What does a man want?

Power. The men spread, the thought extends. I paint
them out, I paint them in again. A blur of forces.
Why take more than we need? Because we can.
Deep footprint, it leaves a hole. You'd break your
heart to make it bigger, so why not crack your skull

when the mind swells. A thought bigger than your
own head. Try it. Seriously. Cover more ground.
I thought of myself as a city and I licked my lips.
I thought of myself as a nation and I wrung my hands,
I put a thing in your hand. Will you defend yourself?

From me, I mean. Let's kill something. The mind
moves forward, the paint layers up: glop glop and
shellac. I shovel the color into our faces, I shovel our
faces into our faces. They look like me. I move them
around. I prefer to blame others, it's easier. King me.

LANDSCAPE WITH FRUIT ROT AND MILLIPEDE

I cut off my head and threw it in the sky. It turned
into birds. I called it thinking. The view from above—
untethered scrutiny. It helps to have an anchor
but your head is going somewhere anyway. It's a matter
of willpower. O little birds, you flap around and

make a mess of the milk-blue sky—all these ghosts
come streaming down and sometimes I wish I had
something else. A redemptive imagination, for
example. The life of the mind is a disappointment,
but remember what stands for what. We deduce

backward into first causes—stone in the pond of things,
splash splash—or we throw ourselves into the future.
We all move forward anyway. Ripples in all directions.
What is a ghost? Something dead that seems to be
alive. Something dead that doesn't know it's dead.

A painting, for instance. An abstraction. *Cut off your
head, kid. For all the good it'll do ya.* I glued my head back
on. All thoughts finish themselves eventually. I wish
it were true. Paint all the men you want but sooner or
later they go to ground and rot. The mind fights the

body and the body fights the land. It wants our bodies,
the landscape does, and everyone runs the risk of
being swallowed up. Can we love nature for what it
really is: predatory? We do not walk through a passive
landscape. The paint dries eventually. The bodies

decompose eventually. We collide with place, which
is another name for God, and limp away with a
permanent injury. Ask for a blessing? You can try,
but we will not remain unscathed. Flex your will
or abandon your will and let the world have its way

with you, or disappear and save everyone the bother
of a dark suit. Why live a life? Well, why are you
asking? I put on my best shirt because the painting
looked so bad. Color bleeds, so make it work for you.
Gravity pulls, so make it work for you. Rubbing

your feet at night or clutching your stomach in the
morning. It was illegible—no single line of sight,
too many angles of approach, smoke in the distance.
It made no sense. When you have nothing to say,
set something on fire. A blurry landscape is useless.

BIRDS HOVER THE TRAMPLED FIELD

I saw them hiding in the yellow field, crouching low
in the varnished dark. I followed them pretending
they were me because they were. I wanted to explain
myself to myself in an understandable way. I gave
shape to my fears and made excuses. I varied my
velocities, watched myselves sleep. Something's not
right about what I'm doing but I'm still doing it—
living in the worst parts, ruining myself. My inner life
is a sheet of black glass. If I fell through the floor
I would keep falling. The enormity of my desire
disgusts me. I kissed my mouth, it was no longer
a mouth. I threw a spear at my head, I didn't have
a head. Fox. At the throat of. The territory is more
complex than I supposed. What does a body of
knowledge look like? A body, any body. Look away
but I'm still there. Birds flying but I'm still there,
lurk there. Not just one of me but multitudes in
the hayfield. Want something to chase you? Run.
Take a body, dump it, drive. Take a body, maybe
your own, and dump it gently. All your dead,
unfinished selves and dump them gently. Take only
what you need. The machine of the world—if you
don't grab on, you begin to tremble. And if you do
grab on, then everything trembles. I spent my lamp
and cleft my head. Deep-wounded mind, I wasn't
doing anything with it anyway. And the birds looking
for a place to land. I would like to say something
about grace, and the brown corduroy thrift store coat
I bought for eight-fifty when you told me my
paintings were empty. Never finish a war without
starting another. I've seen your true face: the back
of your head. If you were walking away, keep walking.

DETAIL OF THE HAYFIELD

I followed myself for a long while, deep into the field.
Two heads full of garbage.

Our scope was larger than I realized,
which only made me that much more responsible.

Yellow, yellow, gold, and ocher.
We stopped. We held the field. We stood very still.

Everyone needs a place.

You need it for the moment you need it, then you bless it—
thank you soup, thank you flashlight—

and move on. Who does this? No one.

THE LANGUAGE OF THE BIRDS

I

A man saw a bird and found him beautiful. The bird had a song inside him, and feathers. Sometimes the man felt like the bird and sometimes the man felt like a stone—solid, inevitable—but mostly he felt like a bird, or that there was a bird inside him, or that something inside him was like a bird fluttering. This went on for a long time.

2

A man saw a bird and wanted to paint it. The problem, if there was one, was simply a problem with the question. Why paint a bird? Why do anything at all? Not how, because hows are easy—series or sequence, one foot after the other—but existentially why bother, what does it solve?

And just because you want to paint a bird, do actually paint a bird, it doesn't mean you've accomplished anything. Who gets to measure the distance between experience and its representation? Who controls the lines of inquiry? We do. Anyone can.

Blackbird, he says. So be it, indexed and normative. But it isn't a bird, it's a man in a bird suit, blue shoulders instead of feathers, because he isn't looking at a bird, real bird, as he paints, he is looking at his heart, which is impossible.

Unless his heart is a metaphor for his heart, as everything is a metaphor for itself, so that looking at the paint is like looking at a bird that isn't there, with a song in its throat that you don't want to hear but you paint anyway.

The hand is a voice that can sing what the voice will not, and the hand wants to do something useful. *Sometimes, at night, in bed, before I fall asleep, I think about a poem I might write, someday, about my heart,* says the heart.

3

They looked at the animals. They looked at the walls of the cave. This is earlier, these are different men. They painted in torchlight: red mostly, sometimes black— mammoth, lion, horse, bear   things on a wall, in profile or superimposed, dynamic and alert.

They weren't animals but they looked like animals, enough like animals to make it confusing, meant something but the meaning was slippery: it wasn't there but it remained, looked like the thing but wasn't the thing—was a second thing, following a second set of rules—and it was too late: their power over it was no longer absolute.

What is alive and what isn't and what should we do about it? Theories: about the nature of the thing. And of the soul. Because people die. The fear: that nothing survives. The greater fear: that something does.

The night sky is vast and wide.

They huddled closer, shoulder to shoulder, painted themselves in herds, all together and apart from the rest. They looked at the sky, and at the mud, and at their hands in the mud, and their dead friends in the mud. This went on for a long time.

4

To be a bird, or a flock of birds doing something to-gether, one or many, starling or murmuration. To be a man on a hill, or all the men on all the hills, or half a man shivering in the flock of himself. These are some choices.

The night sky is vast and wide.

A man had two birds in his head—not in his throat, not in his chest—and the birds would sing all day nev-er stopping. The man thought to himself, *One of these birds is not my bird.* The birds agreed.

STILL LIFE WITH SKULLS AND BACON

A thing and a thing and a thing held still—
you have to hold something still to find the other
things. This is speculation. You will die in your
sleep and leave everything unfinished. This is
also speculation. I had obligations: hope, but hope
negates the experience. I owe myself nothing.
I cut off my head and threw it on the ground.
I walked away. This is how we measure, walking
away. We carve up the world into feet and minutes,
to know how far from home, how many hogs
in the yard. My head just sat there. Fair enough.
A map without landmarks is useless. Science
dreams its dreams of knowledge—names it, pokes it
with equations. The crucial thing is not fifty
times whatever but how we got these notions: how
much, how many, how far, how long. It's good
to give explicit answers, showing all the steps,
necessary and sufficient. Finding the dots,
connecting the dots. An interrogation of the dots.
A pip, a point, a seed, a stone. This is philosophy.
These are suppositions. If one has no apples,
one has zero apples. There is, you see, no shortage
of open problems. We carve up the world
and crown it with numbers—lumens, ounces,
decibels. All these things and what to do with them.
We carve up the world all the time.

LANDSCAPE WITH SEVERAL SMALL FIRES

I like dead things, says the landscape. *They cannot
hurt me.* The armies swarm the cities of the yellow field
and burn them down. *There's not enough room for us
to be ourselves,* say the soldiers streaming across
the plains. *So you will have to be pushed out of the way.*

We like things related to our survival: soup, arrows—
they expand the range of the species. Goldmine,
goldmine, landmine. War, and the art of war, and the
landscape of war. *Grant me freedom from objects,*
says the painting. *I will help you,* says the paint.

More territories. We sat in our tanks and rolled
over our enemies. We trampled everything into
noise and mud. Willpower, gunpowder, concussive
thunder. Pink, orange, red, orange dreaming red.
I am the fire, says the fire. *My body is a graveyard,*

says the landscape. *You're welcome,* says the landscape.
Gold bodies on the red, red ground. I paint in
the wounds. *Socket,* says the shoulder. *Shoulder,* says
the socket. *Let's kill everything,* says everything else.
Smeared night, smudged dawn, I saw him fall. Them,

falling. Split and felled and pounded into the ground.
We knocked the heads off the statuary, deprived
the landmarks of any meaning. Victory swelling
in the occupation. History is painted by the winners.
Keep your paints wet. Trust me, I have things to say.

DETAIL OF THE FIRE

A man with a bandage is in the middle of something.
Everyone understands this. Everyone wants a battlefield.

Red. And a little more red.

Accidents never happen when the room is empty.
Everyone understands this. Everyone needs a place.

People like to think war means something.

What can you learn from your opponent? More than you think.
Who will master this love? Love might be the wrong word.

Let's admit, without apology, what we do to each other.
We know who our enemies are. We know.

I

Two rabbits were chased by a fox, of all the crazy shit in the world, and the fox kept up the chase, circling the world until the world caught up with them in some broken-down downtown metropolis. Inside the warren, the rabbits think fast. Pip touches the only other rabbit listening.

Pip: We're doomed.
Flip: We're not.
Pip: Are you sure?
Flip: Yes. Here, hide inside me.

This is the story of Pip and Flip, the bunny twins. We say that once there were two and now there is only one. When the fox sees Pip run past, he won't know that the one is inside the other. He'll think, *Well, there's at least one more rabbit in that warren.* But no one's left. You know this and I know this. Together we trace out the trail away from doom. There isn't hope, there is a trail. I follow you.

When a rabbit meets a rabbit, one takes the time to tell the other this story. The rabbits then agree there must be two rabbits, at least two rabbits, and that in turn there is a trace. I am only repeating what I heard. This is one love. There are many loves but only one war.

Bird 1: This is the same story.
Bird 2: No, this is the rest of the story.

2

Let me tell you a story about war. A man found his life to be empty. He began to study Latin. Latin was difficult for the man to understand. *I will study Latin, even though it is difficult,* said the man. *Yes, even if it is difficult.*

Let me tell you a story about war. A man had a dream about a woman and then he met her. The man had a dream about the woman's former lover. The former lover was sad, he wanted to fight. The man said to the woman, *I will have to comfort your former lover or I will always be fighting him in my dreams. Yes,* said the woman. *You will need to comfort him, or we will never be finished with this.*

Let me tell you a story about war. A fisherman's son and his dead brother sat on the shore. *That is my country and this is your country and the line in the sand is the threshold between them,* said the dead brother. *Yes,* said the fisherman's son.

You cannot have an opponent if you keep saying yes.

Bird 1: This is the wrong story.
Bird 2: All stories are the wrong story when you are impatient.

Let me tell you a story about war. A man says to another man, *Can I tell you something?* The other man says, *No.* A man says to another man, *There is something I have to tell you. No,* says the other man. *No, you don't.*

Bird 1: Now we are getting somewhere.
Bird 2: Yes, yes we are.

3

Let me tell you a story about war:

A boy spills a glass of milk and his father picks him up by the back of the shirt and throws him against the wall. *You killed my wife and you can't even keep a glass on the table.* The wife had died of sadness, by her own hand. The father walks out of the room and the room is almost empty.

The road outside the house lies flat on the ground. The ground surrenders.

The father works late. The dead wife's hand makes fishsticks while the boy sits in the corner where he fell. The fish in the fishsticks think to themselves, *This is not what we meant to be.*

Its roots in the ground and its branches in the air, a tree is pulled in two directions.

The wife has a dead hand. This is earlier. She is living and her dead hand feeds her pills that don't work. The boy sleeps on the roof or falls out of trees. The father works late. The wife looks out the window and thinks, *Not this.*

The boy is a bird, bad bird. He falls out of trees.

4

Let me tell you a story about war:

The fisherman's son serves drinks to sailors. He stands behind the bar. He listens closely for news of his dead brother. The sailors are thirsty. They drink rum. *Tell me a story,* says the fisherman's son.

There is nothing interesting about the sea. The water is flat, flat and calm, it seems a sheet of glass. You look at it, the more you look at it the more you feel like you are looking into your own head, which is a stranger's head, empty. We listen to the sound with our equipment. I have learned to understand this sound. When you look there is nothing, with the equipment there is sound. We sit in rows and listen down the tunnels for the song. The song has red words in it. We write them down on sheets of paper and pass them along. Sometimes there is noise and sometimes song and often there is silence, the long tunnel, the sea like glass...

You are a translator, says the fisherman's son.
Yes, says the sailor.
And the sound is the voice of the enemy.
Yes, yes it is.

5

Let me tell you a story about love:

She had a soft voice and strong hands. When she sang she would seem too large for the room and she would play guitar and sing, which would make his chest feel huge. Sometimes he would touch her knee and smile. Sometimes she would touch his face and close her eyes.

6

The fisherman's son is a spy, a good one. Spies like documents. Spies wander and roam, scanning the information.

A man does work. A machine can, too. Power of agency, agent of what? This is a question we might ask.

What is a document before it's a document? A noise in your head, a backstory. What makes a thing yours to steal or sell or trade? That is a question, good question.

Spies are pollinators. They take the bits from here and there to make a new thing grow. Does it matter to which team this new thing belongs?

7

Fox rounds the warren but there are no bunnies, jumps up with claws but there are no bunnies, moves down the road but there are no bunnies. There are no bunnies. He chases a bird instead. All wars are the same war. The bird flies away.

8

The fisherman's son knows nothing worth stealing. Perhaps, perhaps.

He once put a cat in a cardboard box, but she got out anyway. He once had a brother he lost to the sea. Brother, dead brother, who speaks to him in dreams. These are a few things worth saying.

He knows that when you snap a mast it's time to get a set of oars or learn how to breathe underwater. Rely on one thing too long and when it disappears and you have nothing—well, that's just bad planning. It's embarrassing, to think it could never happen. It happens.

You cannot get in the way of anyone's path to God. You can, but it does no good. Every spy knows this. Some say God is where we put our sorrow. God says, *Which one of you fuckers can get to me first?*

9

The spies meet at the chain-link fence and tell each other stories. A whisper system, a level of honesty. To testify against yourself is an interesting thing, a sacrifice. Some people do it. Some people find money in the street, but you can't rely on it. The fisherman's son is at the fence, waiting to see if he is useful.

You cannot get in the way of anyone's path to happiness, it also does no good. The problem is figuring out which part is the path and which part is the happiness.

It's a blessing: every day someone shows up at the fence. And when no one shows up, a different kind of blessing. In the wrong light anyone can look like a darkness.

PORTRAIT OF FRYDERYK IN SHIFTING LIGHT

There is something terribly wrong with his face—
empty, restless, one side older than the other.
What is a thing? Sediment. A slow river clogged with
silt. I sussed the gesso into foam and white roses,
stalling. I troubled the shadows and silvered his edges.
What can you know about a person? They shift
in the light. You can't light up all sides at once. Add
a second light and you get a second darkness, it's only
fair. He is looking at the wall and I am looking at his
looking. Difficult thing, to be scrutinized so long.
I find the parts that overlap with mine and light them
up in clays and creams, yellow music singing pink,
the flicker of his mouth a purple rust. His face
congeals as he settles in. His hair is bronze in here,
not gold: walnut, bark, and cinnamon, chipped brick
tipped in ink. My shadow falls across his face, blue milk
and pistachio, his eyes shine like wedding rings. My
shadow falls across him and it doesn't go away. Some
hours later the light has shifted, the floorboards
creak. You can't paint the inside of anything, so why
would you try? Painting the inside of anything is
dangerous. I imagined my wrists broken just enough
to keep the feeling from crawling up my arm.
Dangerous thing: an open arm, an open channel.
All these things, rungs of the ladder. Lovers
do the looking while the strangers look away. It isn't
fair, the depth of my looking, the threat of my
looking. It's rude to shake a man visible and claim
the results. This side of his face, now this side of his
face. His profile up against the tulips. I put down
the brush and walked around the room. Even when
I look away I am still looking. He is inside his body
and I am inside my body and it matters less and less.
Shared face, shared looking. A collaboration.
He didn't expect to be handed over, to be delivered. To be

tricked into his own face. Anyone can paint
a mask. It's boring. And everyone secretly wants
to collaborate with the enemy, to construct a truer
version of the self. How much can you change
and get away with it, before you turn into someone
else, before it's some kind of murder? Difficult,
to be confronted with the fact of yourself. Opaque
in the sense of finally solid, in the sense of
see me, not through me. The selves, glaze on glaze,
accumulating their moods and minutes. We tremble
and I paint the trembling. I enlarged his mouth
and everything went blurry, a forgery. It might
as well be. And all my fingers turned to twigs. Inside
himself he jumped a little. Why build a room you
can live in? Why build a shed for your fears?
The life of the body is a nightmare. This is my hand
over his face, which isn't his face anymore, revising.
I made a shape of the shape he made, subtracted
what he shared with anyone else. There wasn't
much left but it felt like him, wild and scared.
It was too much to bear. I put down the brush and
looked at my hands. I turned off the headlights of
my looking and let the animal get away.

THREE PROOFS

Pablo Picasso, *Gertrude Stein,* 1905–6

When she saw herself, finished, she said *It doesn't look like
me.* Picasso said, *It will.* Perhaps it will look like her
because it is the document and will remain, while she is
just a person who will fade. Now, when we think of her,
we think of this painting. Picasso was planning ahead.
The painting is evidence but not proof. There's no proof
that she looked like that, even though we have the
document. She existed enough to be painted. She could
have been an idea, but that's another kind of existing.
The hand is a tool. The brush is a tool. The paint as well.
There is no machine here, though the work gets done.
A hammer is a tool when banging its head but a lever
when pulling up nails. A lever is a machine, has a fulcrum
which can be moved to change the ratio of something
or other, effort for distance. There is a fulcrum in
the mind that can be moved as well. I do not know what
else to say about this.

Raphael, *Saint George and the Dragon,* 1504–6

It's hard to talk about what you believe while you are
believing it. Fervor reduces thought to shorthand and
all we get is an icon. Give a man a weapon and you
have a warrior. Put him on a horse and you have
a hero. The weapon is a tool. The horse is a metaphor.
Raphael painted this twice—white horse facing east
against the greens, white horse facing west against the
yellows. The maiden flees or prays, depending. A basic
dragon, the kind you'd expect from the Renaissance.
Evidence of evil but not proof. There's a companion
piece as well: *Saint Michael.* Paint angels, it's easier:
you don't need the horse. Michael stands on Satan's
throat, vanquishing, while everything brown burns red.

All these things happened. Allegedly. When you paint
an evil thing, do you invoke it or take away its power?
This has nothing to do with faith but is still a good
question. Raphael was trying to say something about
spirituality. This could be the definition of painting.
The best part of spirituality is reverence. There are other
parts. Some people like to hear the sound of their own
voice. If you don't believe in the world it would be
stupid to paint it. If you don't believe in God, then who
are you talking to?

Caravaggio, *David with the Head of Goliath*, 1609–10

Wanted for murder, a price on his head, Caravaggio
does what he always does—he tries to paint his
way out of it. This bad boy—whose moodiness came
to be called the Baroque, this thug whose soul
was as big as Rome and full of anvils—paints his own
face on Goliath's severed head and offers himself up
as villain, captured, to escape the hammers of the law.
Allegory, yes. A truth as well. But truth doesn't count
in law, only proof. He took the gods and made them
human. His Bacchus was a worn-out drunk. An animal
likely to sleep in a pool of its own sick. He raised
the status of the still life, made subjects out of objects,
turned nature into drama—the bloom on the grapes,
the bloom on the boys, leaves as important as
nudes. Exaggerated light, pure theater. Evidence
of a mind he delights in. Evicted from Rome, he wants
back in. They want his head and he's prepared to
give it to them. He paints David in yellow pants while
the pope's nephew arranges his pardon. July 1610—
Caravaggio rolls up his paintings and sets sail from
Naples, heading north. They stop for supplies. No
one's heard of the pardon. Jail. He pays his way out,
but the boat and his paintings have sailed on without
him. He follows. Malaria. He dies three days before

his pardon arrives and three days after Rembrandt's
fourth birthday. His painted head arrives in Rome weeks
later. All painting is sent downstream, into the future.

René Magritte, *La Clairvoyance*, 1936

Odin had ravens. Zeus was a swan. Magritte saw an egg
and painted a bird. Part of heroism is being able to
see the future and still remain standing. If you don't
believe in God or Fate you still must believe in narrative.
I am waiting for you, here in the trainstation, says the
trainstation. Philosophy is thinking. Prophecy is wishful
thinking. It's easy to find evidence of the future but
harder to make people believe you. This is only obvious
if you have tried. Odin had proxies. Zeus had disguises.
Magritte saw the back of his head in a mirror. Not
hindsight, not really. A debriefing. He claimed that an
image was treacherous. He was right about that but
he might not have understood directionality. His paintings,
though mysterious, conceal nothing. A possible world
and its incomprehensibilities. A purposeful distortion.
Dreaming in the service of. True in the sense of carpentry.

GHOST, ZERO, SUITCASE, AND THE MOON

Contrast and likeness, the difference between
one bird and many. The similarity of one bird, one
worm, one stone. From finger-counting to sticks,
to symbols, to abstractions: magnitudes no longer
represented by pebbles. Numbers larger than ten

are no longer human: they fly from the hand into
the imaginary sky we call hypothesis. Take this
bird, for example: make it equal something. Get it on
one side of the sky. Solve means isolate. Solve means
conquer. The numbers suit up and take the field.

Was I discovered or invented? asks the zero. *Feels like
I've always been here.* I put a line around his border
but he still wasn't there. A hole in the world. A failure.
I turned away. *You start counting at one, not zero,
which is wrong,* says the moon. Thing or nothing,

where or nowhere. *Measure yourself against the truth and
not the other way around,* says the ghost. Man, moon,
ghost, zero—naming rounds off. Perfect and
completely dead. *Your math is crazy,* says the moon.
You can count to eight with the spaces between your

fingers, says the ghost. *If you have one apples and
I take away one apples you have, zero apples and a sadness,*
says the sadness. *It's true,* says eleven, putting on
his suit. *Counting is boring, even when it works,* says
the square root of negative one. *Subtraction is worse,* says

the ghost while the sadness nods his head. *Math is just
replacing things with other things,* says the moon.
Skull on a bottle equals poison, says the moon. *We erase
birds from the sky in an attempt to solve for, we put
bodies in piles in an attempt to solve for,* says the ghost.

*People don't learn anything unless they are afraid of
being left behind,* says the suitcase. *I am afraid,* says the
suitcase. Here and there and what to do about it. *Leave
out the equal sign and the very idea of place will end,*
says the equal sign. *Even when you are in rocketships.*

Black ice in moonlight. A spiritual algebra. Zero zero
zero roses. *And I am not the moon,* says the moon.
I am your own big stupid head just trying to talk to you.
A hole in the sky and we call it the moon. *You are bound
to have many questions now. Try to formulate them.*

LOGIC

A clock is a machine. A gear is a tool. There is rarely
any joy in a frictionless place, so find your inner viscosity.
The mind says viscosity is resistance to flow. The body
puts glue on a twig and catches a bird. Glue is a tool,
unless you are a bird. If you are a bird, then glue is
an inconvenience. A tool does work. A bird flies away
from danger and lands where it can. All thinking is
comparison. A bear is a weapon, a bear claw is a pastry.
A bear trap, if you are a bear, is an inconvenience.
Logic is boring because it works. Being unreasonable is
exciting. Machines have knobs you can turn if you
want to. A hammer is a hammer when it hits the nail.
A hammer is not a hammer when it is sleeping. I woke
up tired of being the hammer. There's a dream in the
space between the hammer and the nail: the dream of
about-to-be-hit, which is a bad dream, but the nail will
take the hit if it gets to sleep inside the wood forever.
I taped a sword to my hand when I was younger. This
is an argument about goals.

LOVESONG OF THE SQUARE ROOT OF NEGATIVE ONE

I am the wind and the wind is invisible, all the leaves
tremble but I am invisible, bloom without flower, knot
without rope, song without throat in wingless flight, dark
boat in the dark night, pure velocity. As the hammer is
a hammer when it hits the nail, and the nail is a nail when
it meets the wood, and the invisible table begins to appear
out of mind, pure mind, out of nothing, pure thinking.
Through darkness, through silence, a vector, a violence,
I labor, I lumber, I fumble forward through the valley as
winter, as water, I mist and frost, flexible and elastic to
the task. I am the hand that lifts the rock, I am the mind
that strings the worm and throws the line and feels the tug,
the flex in the pole, and foot by foot I find the groove,
the trace in the thicket, the key in the lock, as root breaks
rock, from seed to flower to fruit to rot, a holy pilgrim
moving through the stations of the yardstick. I track,
I follow, I hinge and turn, frictionless and efficient as an
equal sign. I flip and fold, I superimpose, I become
location and you veer toward me, the eye to which you
are relative, magnetized for your revelation. Hook and bait,
polestar and checkmate, I am your arrival, there is no
refusal, we are here, you see, together, we are already here.

THE FIELD OF ROOMS AND HALLS

I

A man found a door and hung it on the wall.

I think he thought in rectangles, each day's bright panel
pushed one against the next, a calendar of light. He
would paint them, all these days, and hang them out
of order: an unreliable hotel where no one ever knew
which rooms were his, which rooms he had actually
been inside of. There were gaps, of course, and some-
times overlaps: days too small to fill their slots, days too
large for the day to hold them. And days, no matter
what their size, that leaked into the next. A leaky day is
a dangerous thing. January and her thirty-two rooms.

2

I put my sadness in a box. The box went soft and wet
and weak at the bottom. I called it Thursday. Today is
Sunday. The town is empty.

I stood in the road looking forward and back, to see if
it would change something. After a while, I went back
inside and tripped over the box.

3

Hard to say, even now, what it was, this extra room. He
put his foot in the door of it, kept it open. He painted
himself and others appeared. He painted his hunger
and suddenly table, the soup fully illustrated in the
depth of its bowl. He used the wrong colors to make
it right, selecting them for what they felt not what
they said, so that everything became a set of relations

outside the realm of simple minutes and their named accumulations. *Bruising Day, The Month of Pears, The Year of Infestations.*

4

Today is Monday. The box is still leaking. Now it is Tuesday.

5

The walls were strong, the nails: reliable. The room grew darker or lighter than it should have been, given the placement of the lamps; the hands of his hands alluding to a secret world beyond the frame he shouldn't have any knowledge of. What's better than a thought? A method. And a hallway appears because you are looking for it.

Each day another panel to lather the paint on, to hide the stone in. Where to place the stone? Inside today, inside tomorrow. Is it the frame that makes it dangerous? There are frames around everything already.

6

The directors agreed. The crates arrived. They added the pieces to the collection and the whole museum shifted. You have to understand it as it is. Shining blue, shining green. This is also part of the story: how the story changes. This is something I forgot to tell you.

THE MYSTERY OF THE PEARS

I looked at the pears. I painted the pears, what they
were like. I waited for the pears to reveal their
mystery. Five brown pears in a chipped white bowl,
soft and scarred and blushing yellow in the throbbing
dark. They shine in their suits. I hung them on
the wall. Precise. A landmark. You might like it here.
I think that you might like it here.

DOTS EVERYWHERE

I erased my legs and forgot to draw in the stilts.
It looks like I'm floating but I'm not floating.
Sometimes I draw you with fangs. I tell you these
things because I love you. Some people paint
with whiskey and call it social drinking. Some people
paint drunk and put dots of color everywhere.
In the morning the dots make them happy. I am
putting dots of color everywhere and you are sleeping.
Something has happened in the paint tonight and
it is worth keeping. It's nothing like I thought it
would be and closer to what I meant. *None of it is
real, darling.* I say it to you. Maybe we will wake up
singing. Maybe we will wake up to the silence
of shoes at the foot of the bed not going anywhere.

THE MUSEUM

Two lovers went to the museum and wandered the
rooms. He saw a painting and stood in front of it
for too long. It was a few minutes before she
realized he had gotten stuck. He was stuck looking
at a painting. She stood next to him, looking at his
face and then the face in the painting. *What do you
see?* she asked. *I don't know,* he said. He didn't
know. She was disappointed, then bored. He was
looking at a face and she was looking at her watch.
This is where everything changed. There was now
a distance between them. He was looking at a face
but it might as well have been a cabbage or a
sugar beet. Perhaps it was something about yellow
near pink. He didn't know how to say it. Years later
he still didn't know how to say it, and she was gone.

THE STAG AND THE QUIVER

1

Once there was a deer called stag. A white breasted, a many pointed. He refused to still when he halted, the hooves in his mind were always lifted. Everything comes close, the branches slide. In a clearing made of cleavings, stag sees another stag. They watch each other, they share no story. *I will not cross you and you must move on. There is nothing else.* It reminds me of some tale, stay with me to remember, it reminds me of where I was going without you.

2

The hunter sinks his arrows into the trees and then paints the targets around them. The trees imagine they are deer. The deer imagine they are safe. The arrows: they have no imagination.

All night the wind blows through the trees. It makes a sound.

The hunter's son watches the hunter. The hunter paints more rings on his glasses. *Everything is a target,* says the hunter. *No matter where you look.* The hunter's son says nothing, and closes his eyes.

3

The hunter's son watches the stag.

Clench is a hand word. His hand is clenched. Door with a bad hinge, it wouldn't open. *Do not let go of the arrow, let it slip through your fingers as you relax your grip.* This is good advice. He couldn't do it. There is no way to get to the future from here.

The key to archery is sustained attention. An arrow is a stick with feathers, an extension of the mind. Men and their thoughts, their quivers and their arrows: it helps to see how these things move, and where they land.

The stag watches the hunter's son.

4

This is a story of loops, at least one. I stepped off the loop. I spent time listening, testing realms. I snapped a twig in my head and struck out. You know what it's like to be alone: gimlets and vermicide. You know what it's like to be alive, so forgiveness.

All night the trees stand silent in the dark, not touching.

I put on the deer suit. I turned my ears in all directions. I'll live alone or in between. This is the testimony of the deer: solitude, the long corridors, love from a distance. You asked me once, *What are we made of?* Well, these are the things we're made of. One house, two house. The road goes away from here.

DETAIL OF THE WOODS

I looked at all the trees and didn't know what to do.

A box made out of leaves.
What else was in the woods? A heart, closing. Nevertheless.

Everyone needs a place. It shouldn't be inside of someone else.
I kept my mind on the moon. Cold Moon, Long Nights Moon.

From the landscape: a sense of scale.
From the dead: a sense of scale.

I turned my back on the story. A sense of superiority.
Everything casts a shadow.

Your body told me in a dream it's never been afraid of anything.

LANDSCAPE WITH BLACK COATS IN SNOW

A door had been opened and could not be shut and then
it was shut. I turned my back and felt the vacuum of
my leaving. I live in big spaces, so I'm left alone in big spaces.
Thinking in the language of the enemy. Moving through
the landscape of the enemy. We were spies and the confidants

of spies, pockets and telephones, gathering evidence without
leaving any. Spies feel like they know something important.
It is a feeling. Opulent. Grand. We invented a fence in the
middle of the snow so we could meet at the fence and whisper.
Clemency at the fence. These small repeated revelations

stabilize something. Faith in snow, bravery in snow. A daily
maintenance. *Is this your sadness?* asks the trashman. No, that
is a fishbone and that is a soup can and that over there is no
longer recognizable. Paint ghosts over everything, the sadness
of everything. We made ourselves cold. We made ourselves

snow. We smuggled ourselves into ourselves. Haunted by
each other's knowledge. To hide somewhere is not surrender,
it is trickery. All day the snow falls down, all night the snow.
I try to guess your trajectory and end up telling my own story.
We left footprints in the slush of ourselves, getting out of there.

SELF-PORTRAIT AGAINST RED WALLPAPER

Close the blinds and kill the birds, I surrender
my desire for a logical culmination. I surrender my
desire to be healed. The blurriness of being alive.
Take it or leave it, and for the most part you take it.
Not just the idea of it but the ramifications of it.
People love to hate themselves, avoiding the
necessary recalibrations. Shame comes from vanity.
Shame means you're guilty, like the rest of us,
but you think you're better than we are. Maybe you
are. What would a better me paint? There is no
new me, there is no old me, there's just me, the same
me, the whole time. Vanity, vanity, forcing your
will on the world. Don't try to make a stronger wind,
you'll wear yourself out. Build a better sail. You
want to solve something? Get out of your own way.
What's the difference between me and the world?
Compartmentalization. The world doesn't know
what to do with my love. Because it isn't used to
being loved. It's a framework problem. Disheartening?
Obviously. I hope it's love. I'm trying really hard
to make it love. I said no more severity. I said it severely
and slept through all my appointments. I clawed
my way into the light but the light is just as scary.
I'd rather quit. I'd rather be sad. It's too much work.
Admirable? Not really. I hate my friends. And when
I hate my friends I've failed myself, failed to share
my compassion. I shine a light on them of my own
making: septic, ugly, the wrong yellow. I mean, maybe
it's better if my opponent wins.

GLUE

I stepped out so things could progress without me.
The knot of the self: take it out. The knot of the self:
what is the rope? The ability to nullify the self
in favor of the landscape, or a lover, or a bowl of fruit.
What happens when I no longer want to meet you?

Something interesting. A legitimate answer, but
it leaves a hole. Nothing lasts forever: we know this.
Looking changes the looker: we know this. It's easier
to talk about one thing at a time: I know, I know.
Mortal love? Sure. Lovers abandoned and desperate?

Sure. Longing and suffering? Of course, of course.
You want it to mean something. Sad pink cakes.
Five strange blue things. You want to have it glued
together. *The days were short and the halls were long.*
Something like that. Crawled up the pleat of my coat:

a shadow did. Shut the basement door: a ghost did.
It accumulates. Grounding the abstract offers several
pleasures: certainly. Love, maybe love, maybe
bathtub: certainly. Grabbing the throat of it: that's
what we always do. You can disconnect it or you can

try to glue it all together. He could glue it all together.
I could. Who's speaking anyway? *Not really a problem,*
says the moon. *Since y'all look the same from up here.*
We could pull it apart, spend our whole lives pulling it
apart and have no time left to do anything smart with

the pieces. The wrong things have been wired
together. Things that shouldn't touch. The sooner
you embrace it, the sooner it will leave you. Okay.
The bruise: milk-yellow. You are what you cover up.
Okay, okay. These damages are connected. I glued

more pictures to it: doctored, rigged, unverifiable.
There were boxes in my head and I moved them
around, pretended it changed something.
It didn't work. I plugged my cord to see
what kind of lamp I was. It didn't matter.

What is a ghost? What is a painting? Yes and yes,
the same answers. My mind wanted a reward, so
it filled in all the gaps it found, smoothed it all out.
I lost the important parts and I set about restoring.
Wanting to show and not being able. Sometimes

the wing of the bird and sometimes the bird
trying to fly. The bird eats worms. At least that
one pure thing. Put yourself in the painting:
you are responsible. Broadcast from a smeary place:
you are responsible. Wearing your dead face,

your man face, your real face: you are responsible.
Clomp clomp down the mines of thinking—
the compromise: where the thought wants to go
and where you want it to go. Truth is relative
to the model: big deal. Mathematicians extend

the natural language: big deal. Precision is necessary
so we can know what we are investigating. Yes, yes:
show me. What holds it together? Glue, some kind
of glue. The image remains as a body would. I turned
the image over like a rock, but then the worms.

TURPENTINE

It is too heavy, says the canvas. *You lack restraint.*
I was sleeping in whiteness, drifts of snow,
and you woke me and told me your dream, my blank
face upturned, listening. You came to me while we
were sleeping, we were both sleeping, and you asked me
to hold this for you. I am holding this for you.

THE STORY OF THE MOON

Once, night, unchallenged, extended its dark grace
across the sky. To the credit of the town, the stars
at night had been enough, though sometimes
the townspeople went about bumping their heads
in sleep. Eventually, three brothers, traveling through
a foreign town, found an evening that did not
disappear behind the mountains, for a shining globe
sat in an oak tree. The brothers stopped. *That one
is the moon,* said a man from the foreign town.
The brothers conferred. They could make certain use
of it. The brothers stole the moon down and put it
in their wagon. Seized it. Thieved its silver. Altogether
greedy. The wagon shining bright. At home:
the moon delivered. Then, celebration: dancing in red
coats on the meadow. Number four brother smiling
wide. The moon installed—it extended its silver
calculations. Time and more time. The brothers aged,
took sick, petitioned the town that each quarter
of the moon, as it was their property, be portioned out
to share their graves. Done, and the light of the moon
diminished in fractions. They had extinguished it,
part for part, and night, unimpeded, fell. Altogether
lanternless. The people were silent. The dark rang loud.
Underground: cold blazing. The dead woke, shivering
in the light. Some went out to play and dance,
others hastened to the taverns to drink, quarrel,
and brawl. Noise and more noise. Noise up to heaven.
Saint Peter took his red horse through the gates
and came down. The moon, for the third time, taken.
The dead bidden back into their graves. One wonders
why a story like this exists.

THE WORM KING'S LULLABY

1

The holes in this story are not lamps, they are not wheels. I walked and walked, grew a beard so I could drag it in the dirt, into a forest that wasn't there. I want to give you more but not everything. You don't need everything.

2

This is what they found on the dead man's desk when the landlord let them in: twenty-eight pages, esoteric and unfollowable, written with perfect penmanship and a total disregard for any reader, as if the intended audience was a population not quite human. *Angelic script,* says the detective, lifting the pages, feeling their heft, and he wonders what he means because it isn't. His partner nods but ignores him.

A park bench, white roses, dark coats and white roses, snow and repetitions of snow—it's hard to read but pretty much how they found him: dead on a bench in a black coat, the snow falling down.

Twigs and blackbirds, snow and red horses, the ghosts floating up, the snow falling down—the detective is weeping—and the black coat.

3

Someone has to leave first. This is a very old story. There is no other version of this story.

4

It's getting late, Little Moon. Finish the song. It's not that late. *You are my moon, Little Moon, and it's late enough. So climb down out of the tree.* Is it safe? *Safe enough.* Are you dead as well?

The night is cold, it is silver, it is a coin.

Not everyone is dead, Little Moon. But the big moon needs the tree. There is a ghost at the end of the song. *Yes, there is. And you see his hand and then you see the moon.* Am I the ghost at the end of the song? *We are very close now, Little Moon. Thank you for shining on me.*

5

He was pointing at the moon but I was looking at his hand. He was dead anyway, a ghost. I'm surprised I saw his hand at all. All this was prepared for me. All this was set in motion long ago. I live in someone else's future. *I stayed as long as I could,* he said. *Now look at the moon.*

THE PAINTING THAT INCLUDES ALL PAINTING

The central panel now missing—

We all dream of the complete document, the atlas of the idea,
the fish on the table finally gutted—

What does all this love amount to?

Putting down the brush for the last time—

ABOUT THE AUTHOR

Richard Siken's poetry collection *Crush* won the 2004 Yale Series of Younger Poets prize, a Lambda Literary Award, a Thom Gunn Award, and was a finalist for the National Book Critics Circle Award. He is a recipient of a Pushcart Prize, two Arizona Commission on the Arts grants, two Lannan Residencies, and a fellowship from the National Endowment for the Arts.

Lannan Literary Selections

For two decades Lannan Foundation has supported the publication
and distribution of exceptional literary works. Copper Canyon Press
gratefully acknowledges their support.

LANNAN LITERARY SELECTIONS 2015

Michael Dickman, *Green Migraine*

Deborah Landau, *The Uses of the Body*

Camille Rankine, *Incorrect Merciful Impulses*

Richard Siken, *War of the Foxes*

Frank Stanford, *What About This: Collected Poems of Frank Stanford*

RECENT LANNAN LITERARY SELECTIONS FROM
COPPER CANYON PRESS

James Arthur, *Charms Against Lightning*

Mark Bibbins, *They Don't Kill You Because They're Hungry,*
They Kill You Because They're Full

Malachi Black, *Storm Toward Morning*

Marianne Boruch, *Cadaver, Speak*

Jericho Brown, *The New Testament*

Olena Kalytiak Davis, *The Poem She Didn't Write and Other Poems*

Natalie Diaz, *When My Brother Was an Aztec*

Matthew Dickman and Michael Dickman, *50 American Plays*

Kerry James Evans, *Bangalore*

Tung-Hui Hu, *Greenhouses, Lighthouses*

Deborah Landau, *The Last Usable Hour*

Sarah Lindsay, *Debt to the Bone-Eating Snotflower*

Michael McGriff, *Home Burial*

Valzhyna Mort, *Collected Body*

Lisa Olstein, *Little Stranger*

Roger Reeves, *King Me*

Ed Skoog, *Rough Day*

For a complete list of Lannan Literary Selections from
Copper Canyon Press, please visit Partners on our website:
www.coppercanyonpress.org

Poetry is vital to language and living. Since 1972, Copper Canyon Press has published extraordinary poetry from around the world to engage the imaginations and intellects of readers, writers, booksellers, librarians, teachers, students, and donors.

WE ARE GRATEFUL FOR THE MAJOR SUPPORT PROVIDED BY:

THE PAUL G. ALLEN FAMILY FOUNDATION

Lannan

Anonymous

John Branch

Diana Broze

Beroz Ferrell & The Point, llc

Janet and Les Cox

Mimi Gardner Gates

Linda Gerrard and Walter Parsons

Gull Industries, Inc.
on behalf of William and Ruth True

Mark Hamilton and Suzie Rapp

Carolyn and Robert Hedin

Steven Myron Holl

Lakeside Industries, Inc.
on behalf of Jeanne Marie Lee

Maureen Lee and Mark Busto

Brice Marden

Ellie Mathews and Carl Youngmann as
The North Press

H. Stewart Parker

Penny and Jerry Peabody

John Phillips and Anne O'Donnell

Joseph C. Roberts

Cynthia Lovelace Sears and Frank Buxton

The Seattle Foundation

Kim and Jeff Seely

Dan Waggoner

C.D. Wright and Forrest Gander

Charles and Barbara Wright

The dedicated interns and faithful volunteers of Copper Canyon Press

TO LEARN MORE ABOUT UNDERWRITING COPPER CANYON PRESS TITLES,
PLEASE CALL 360-385-4925 EXT. 103

After the great success of *Birds of America*, renowned
ornithologist John James Audubon turned his attention
to viviparous quadrupeds. Difficult, as most are nocturnal.
A few of the animals Audubon illustrated are so-called
"mystery animals" since they still remain unidentified.

The Chinese character for poetry is made up of two parts:
"word" and "temple." It also serves as pressmark for
Copper Canyon Press.

The poems are set in Adobe Garamond.
Book design and composition by Phil Kovacevich.